Incredible Earth

Richard Northcott

OXFORD
UNIVERSITY PRESS

OXFORD
UNIVERSITY PRESS

Great Clarendon Street, Oxford OX2 6DP

Oxford University Press is a department of the University of Oxford. It furthers the University's objective of excellence in research, scholarship, and education by publishing worldwide in

Oxford New York

Auckland Cape Town Dar es Salaam Hong Kong Karachi Kuala Lumpur Madrid Melbourne Mexico City Nairobi New Delhi Shanghai Taipei Toronto

With offices in

Argentina Austria Brazil Chile Czech Republic France Greece Guatemala Hungary Italy Japan Poland Portugal Singapore South Korea Switzerland Thailand Turkey Ukraine Vietnam

OXFORD and OXFORD ENGLISH are registered trade marks of Oxford University Press in the UK and in certain other countries

© Oxford University Press 2010

The moral rights of the author have been asserted

Database right Oxford University Press (maker)

First published 2010
2016 2015 2014
20 19 18 17 16 15 14 13 12

ISBN: 978 0 19 464438 9

An Audio CD Pack containing this book and a CD is also available
ISBN: 978 0 19 464478 5
The CD has a choice of American and British English recordings of the complete text.

An accompanying Activity Book is also available
ISBN: 978 0 19 464448 8

Printed in China
This book is printed on paper from certified and well-managed sources

ACKNOWLEDGEMENTS

Illustrations by: Kelly Kennedy pp 9, 11, 20; Dusan Pavlic/ Beehive Illustration pp 25, 26, 30, 32, 38, 40, 46, 47; Alan Rowe pp 25, 26, 28, 40, 46, 47; Jane Smith pp 4, 18, 19.

The publisher would like to thank the following for their kind permission to reproduce photographs and other copyright material: Alamy pp 3 (Greg Vaughn), 6 (dbimages), 13 (Robert Harding Picture Library/Pamukkale), 17 (Chris Howes/Wild Places Photography/Sarawak Chamber, JUPITERIMAGES/Agence Images/Lascaux), 18 (Hans Westheim Photography), 19 (DEDDEDA); Corbis pp 9 (Layne Kennedy), 11 (Paul Sanders), 12 (Adam Jones), 16 (Robert Dowling), 20 (Kazuyoshi Nomachi), 21 (Peter Adams), 23 (Ron Watts); Getty Images pp 5 (Ralph Lee Hopkins/National Geographic/painted desert), 7 (Jeff Hunter/Photographer's Choice/turtle), 13 (Koichi Kamoshida/monkeys), 14 (Jon Hicks/Photographer's Choice), 15 (Dmitry Kostyukov/AFP), 22 (Daryl Benson); Oxford University Press pp 7 (coral island), 8, 10; Ragnar Th. Sigurdsson/Arctic Images p 5 (Surtsey).

With thanks to Ann Fullick for science checking

Introduction

Don't go near! This is a volcano, and it's erupting. Volcanoes are dangerous, but they are beautiful, too. There are many other incredible places on Earth – high mountains, great rivers, big deserts ...

What is the highest mountain on Earth?
What is the biggest hot desert?
What is the deepest lake?
What incredible places do you know?

Discover!

Now read and discover more about our incredible Earth!

Earth's Crust

Earth is round, like an orange. Oranges have a skin and Earth has a skin, too. We call this skin Earth's crust. Under the crust there is very hot rock.

Earth's crust has different pieces. These pieces move very, very slowly. Millions of years ago, the pieces moved and made mountains. Under mountains the crust is thick, but under the ocean it's thinner. When two pieces of the crust move and meet, there can be earthquakes.

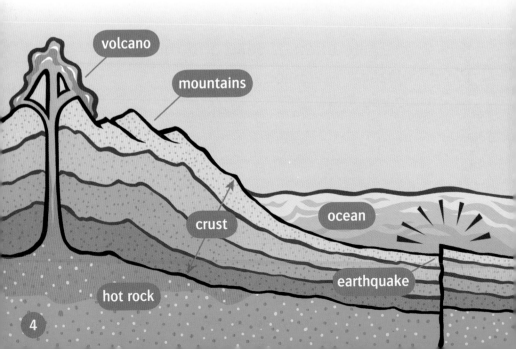

volcano

mountains

crust

ocean

earthquake

hot rock

A volcano is a hole in Earth's crust. When a volcano erupts, hot rock flies out from under the ground, and melted rock pours out over the ground. Volcanoes under the ocean sometimes make new islands. In 1963, a volcano in the Atlantic Ocean made a new island called Surtsey.

Surtsey Island, Iceland

There are many different rocks in Earth's crust. They are millions of years old. The rocks are often different colors. In the Painted Desert in Arizona in the USA, you can see the different rocks.

The Painted Desert, USA

Go to pages 24–25 for activities.

Oceans

On Earth there is more ocean than land. The Pacific Ocean is the biggest ocean. It's bigger than Africa!

Did you know that there are mountains and valleys under the ocean? Some of these mountains are bigger than the biggest mountains on land. In the deepest parts of the ocean, the water is 10 kilometers deep.

The water in the ocean is always moving. Waves hit the land and break the rocks. Sometimes, big pieces of rock fall into the ocean. They leave big cliffs, like the beautiful Uluwatu Cliffs in Bali in Indonesia.

Uluwatu Cliffs, Bali

coral

Great Barrier Reef, Australia

Where the ocean is warm, we sometimes find coral. Coral is made of millions of very small animals that make hard covers around themselves. When the animals die, the hard covers make the coral reef.

The Great Barrier Reef near Australia is the biggest coral reef in the world. It's 2,300 kilometers long. Sea turtles, dolphins, and many other amazing animals live there.

Discover!

In some places, where the coral reef is very big, it comes out of the water. It makes a small island.

Go to pages 26–27 for activities.

3 Rivers and Waterfalls

Rivers usually begin as streams in mountains. The water comes from rain or snow. All rivers then go to the ocean.

Big rivers are very strong. When the ground under a river is soft, the river makes valleys. When the ground under it is hard rock, there are waterfalls or rapids.

One incredible waterfall is the Iguazu Falls between Argentina and Brazil. Iguazu means 'big water' in an old language of South America.

Iguazu Falls, South America

There's more water in the River Amazon than in any other river in the world. It begins in the mountains in Peru and Ecuador. Then it goes through the rainforest in Brazil, and to the Atlantic Ocean.

There are no bridges on the Amazon. First, the river goes through rainforest and there are no roads. Then, near the ocean, the river is very wide so people can't build bridges. They cross the river by boat.

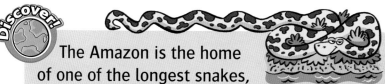

Discover!

The Amazon is the home of one of the longest snakes, called anacondas. Some grow to 9 meters long.

→ Go to pages 28–29 for activities.

9

Glaciers and Icebergs

The coldest places on Earth are in the highest mountains, and at the North and South Poles. Here, there are rivers made of ice. They are called glaciers. Glaciers begin when snow falls.

Mountain glaciers move very, very slowly down the mountain. When the ice melts, the water goes into rivers. It can take thousands of years for the water from a glacier to get to the ocean.

Los Glaciares National Park, Argentina

glacier

Ilulissat, Greenland

At the North and South Poles, where the glaciers are near the ocean, very big pieces of ice break off. These are called icebergs. Icebergs move slowly on the ocean.

Near the North Pole, Ilulissat is one of the most incredible places on Earth – and one of the coldest. The glacier and icebergs here are very, very big. The glacier is about 40 kilometers long and it moves slowly to the Arctic Ocean. It moves about 30 meters every day.

Discover!

Icebergs are dangerous for boats. Most of the ice is under the water, so people in boats can't see all the ice.

→ Go to pages 30–31 for activities.

5 Hot Water

Imagine you are in this park. Suddenly, you hear a loud noise of water moving very fast. Then hot water and steam pour out of the ground. You are looking at a geyser.

What makes a geyser? When it rains or snows, the water goes into the ground. Deep under the ground there is hot rock. If rainwater touches a lot of hot rock, it begins to boil. Then there's a lot of steam.

Suddenly, the water can't stay under the ground. It has to come out. Geysers are very hot, so don't go near them!

A Geyser in Yellowstone National Park, USA

Pamukkale Cliffs, Turkey

These white cliffs look like they are made of ice, but they are really made of rock. Hot water came out of the ground and poured down the mountain. Then minerals in the water made these incredible cliffs. They look like waterfalls, but they never move. They are thousands of years old.

Discover!

At the Jigokudani Monkey Park in Japan, hot water from under the ground makes pools. When the weather is cold, monkeys sit in the warm water.

→ Go to pages 32–33 for activities.

6 Mountains and Lakes

The Himalayas, Asia

The biggest mountain chain in the world is the Himalayas in Asia. It began when two pieces of Earth's crust met and moved up. They began to move about 50 million years ago – and they are moving now, very slowly.

The top of Mount Everest in the Himalayas is the highest place on Earth – it's about 9 kilometers above the ocean. Everest is very big and it's getting bigger. The top of Everest goes up about 5 millimeters every year, because Earth's crust is moving all the time.

Near high mountains there are often deep lakes. The deepest lake in the world is Lake Baikal in Russia. It's more than 1,600 meters deep. Scientists are exploring the lake in small submarines.

Lake Baikal began when pieces of Earth's crust moved and made a deep hole. Water from 330 rivers goes into Lake Baikal. There's more water here than in all the Great Lakes in North America!

On Lake Baikal, Russia

submarine

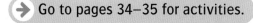

Go to pages 34–35 for activities.

7 Caves

Caves are incredible underground worlds. Many people are interested in them.

What makes a cave? Near the coast, ocean waves hit cliffs and make holes. In the mountains, the moving ice in a glacier makes caves in the rock.

The most incredible caves are in soft rock called limestone. Rain falls on the limestone and makes holes. Slowly, the holes grow bigger and make caves. This takes thousands and thousands of years.

Discover!

The Sarawak Chamber in Borneo is the biggest cave in the world. It's longer than ten big planes!

stalactites

stalagmites

Caves are usually very wet because water comes through the rock. Slowly, the raindrops mix with minerals and build incredible rock sculptures, called stalactites and stalagmites.

Thousands of years ago, people lived in caves. They didn't have books or paper, so they drew pictures on the cave walls. People drew this picture in a cave in France, about 16,000 years ago.

➜ Go to pages 36–37 for activities.

8 Earthquakes and Tsunamis

Usually, Earth's crust moves very slowly – only a few millimeters every year. Sometimes, two pieces of the crust move suddenly in different directions, and then there's an earthquake.

Earthquakes are dangerous because buildings sometimes fall down. When there's an earthquake, people in buildings go under a heavy table. Or they stand between two rooms. These are good ideas – they can help to keep people safe.

After an Earthquake

earthquake

tsunami

earthquake

After a Tsunami

There are earthquakes under the ocean, too. Usually, they are small and not dangerous. Sometimes an earthquake under the ocean makes a giant wave called a tsunami. Tsunamis can be very dangerous.

After a tsunami, there are often floods. There's water everywhere. Houses, cars, and trees are in the water. The water isn't clean, so many people are sick. In 2004, there was a very big tsunami in the Indian Ocean. Many people died.

Go to pages 38–39 for activities.

9 Deserts

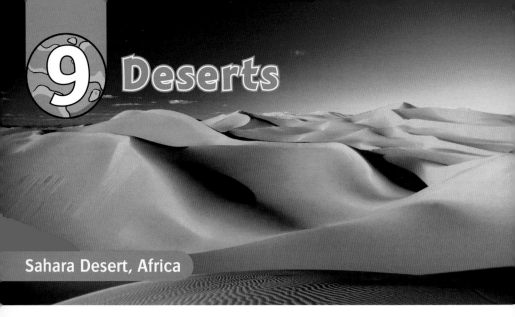

Sahara Desert, Africa

A desert is a dry place, with almost no rain. About 20 percent (%) of the land on Earth is desert. What are deserts made of? Some deserts are made of sand, and many deserts are made of stones or rocks. Deserts are usually hot, but not always. Antarctica is a cold desert. It doesn't rain often there, but there's lots of ice.

The Sahara Desert in Africa is the biggest hot desert on Earth. It's bigger than Australia! The animals in the desert can live there because they don't drink very often.

 Camels can live for a week with no water.

In Bolivia in South America, there's a desert made of salt. It's called the Salar de Uyuni. About 40,000 years ago it was a saltwater lake, but now the ground is hard and dry most of the time. Sometimes the ground looks like a big mirror.

Many people visit the Salar de Uyuni because it's an incredible place. There's even a hotel made of salt!

Salar de Uyuni, Bolivia

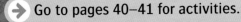

Go to pages 40–41 for activities.

10 Erosion

Cappadocia, Turkey

Where are these rocks? Are they on the moon? No, they are in Cappadocia in Turkey.

They look like sculptures, but no one made them. Really, the windy weather made them. These rocks are not very hard. The wind blows on them and very slowly changes them. When the weather changes Earth in this way, we call it erosion.

In the Colorado River in the USA, erosion began about 20 million years ago. The river moved over the rock and slowly broke it. Sun, cold weather, and wind broke the rock, too. All these things made the incredible deep valley called the Grand Canyon.

Wind, rain, sun, and snow – the weather is a part of Earth's story. Sun and wind make deserts. Glaciers move between mountains and make valleys. Rain falls on limestone and makes caves … This story began millions of years ago, and it is still going on. What an incredible story it is!

The Grand Canyon, USA

 Go to pages 42–43 for activities.

1 Earth's Crust

← Read pages 4–5.

1 Match.

1 Earth is	of years old.
2 Earth's crust is millions	the ocean.
3 The pieces of Earth's crust	in Earth's crust.
4 There are different rocks	round.
5 Under Earth's crust, there's	very hot rock.
6 There are volcanoes under	move very slowly.

2 Complete the sentences.

crust   holes   ocean   ~~old~~   rocks   volcano

1 Some mountains are millions of years _old_.

2 When pieces of Earth's _____ meet, there are sometimes earthquakes.

3 Volcanoes are _____ in Earth's crust.

4 The rock in a _____ is very hot.

5 Sometimes a volcano under the _____ makes a new island.

6 In the Painted Desert the _____ are different colors.

3 Find and write the words.

1 crust

2 _____

3 _____

4 _____

w	a	d	m	i	s	l	a	n	d
z	f	t	o	k	y	b	o	t	b
d	c	r	u	s	t	j	c	s	t
l	E	d	n	r	a	h	e	a	m
e	a	r	t	h	q	u	a	k	e
a	r	r	a	k	l	o	n	e	p
y	t	o	i	m	e	t	v	x	e
p	h	c	n	o	q	o	z	s	n
m	r	k	v	o	l	c	a	n	o
w	c	s	n	u	l	k	q	l	w

5 _____   7 _____

6 _____   8 _____

4 Circle the odd one out.

1 Japan (Earth) Russia China

2 orange   apple   banana   skin

3 move   fall   piece   erupt

4 volcano   dangerous   beautiful   incredible

5 in   under   on   ground

6 red   brown   desert   yellow

2 Oceans

← Read pages 6–7.

1 Write the words.

cliffs   coral   dolphin
sea turtle   ~~valley~~   waves

1 _valley_

2 _____

3 _____

4 _____

5 _____

6 _____

2 Write *true* or *false*.

1 There are mountains under the ocean.   _true_

2 Africa is bigger than the Pacific Ocean.   _____

3 Waves can break rocks.   _____

4 A coral reef can make an island.   _____

5 The Great Barrier Reef is near Africa.   _____

6 Sea turtles live in coral reefs.   _____

3 Answer the questions.

1 What is the biggest ocean on Earth?

   It's the Pacific Ocean.

2 How deep is the deepest water in the ocean?

   _____

3 Where are the Uluwatu Cliffs?

   _____

4 What is coral made of?

   _____

5 Where is the Great Barrier Reef?

   _____

4 Add the words and write correct sentences.

1 The Pacific Ocean is than Africa. (bigger)

   The Pacific Ocean is bigger than Africa.

2 There are big mountains the ocean. (under)

   _____

3 When waves hit the land, rocks into the ocean. (fall)

   _____

4 Coral is hard, it isn't made of rock. (but)

   _____

5 Many amazing animals near coral reefs. (live)

   _____

3 Rivers and Waterfalls

← Read pages 8–9.

1 Write the words.

river   waterfall
mountain   rainforest

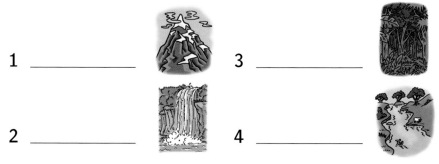

1 _____

2 _____

3 _____

4 _____

2 Circle the correct words.

1 The Iguazu Falls are in **Australia** / (**South America.**)

2 The ground under waterfalls is **hard** / **soft**.

3 The Amazon begins in the **mountains** / **ocean**.

4 The Amazon goes **through** / **under** the rainforest.

5 The **Amazon** / **anaconda** is a very long snake.

3 Circle the odd one out.

1 river   ocean   waterfall   kilometer

2 water   rain   rock   snow

3 snake   waterfall   river   rapids

4 mountain   hard   soft   strong

5 Peru   Ecuador   Amazon   Brazil

4 Write the words.   Amazon   anaconda   Brazil
Iguazu Falls   ocean   rainforest

1 All rivers go here.   the _____

2 This big river is in South America. the _____

3 There are many trees here.   the _____

4 This country is in South America.   _____

5 This is an incredible waterfall.   the _____

6 This is a very long snake.   the _____

5 Write correct sentences.

1 The world in rivers comes from rain or snow.

   The water in rivers comes from rain or snow.

2 When a river goes over rocks, it makes rain.

   _____

3 Iguazu Falls is a South American rainforest.

   _____

4 The Amazon begins in the rainforest in Peru.

   _____

5 The Amazon goes through a big mountain.

   _____

6 You can find rivers in the Amazon.

   _____

4 Glaciers and Icebergs

← Read pages 10–11.

1 Complete the sentences.

glacier   ice   incredible   mountain   slowly   icebergs

1 A _____ is a river made of ice.

2 Glaciers move down the _____ .

3 Glaciers move very, very _____ .

4 Near the ocean, glaciers break and make _____ .

5 In icebergs a lot of _____ is under the water.

6 There are _____ icebergs at Ilulissat.

2 Complete the chart.

coral reef   glacier   ice   iceberg   snow
~~Amazon Rainforest~~   volcano   melted rock

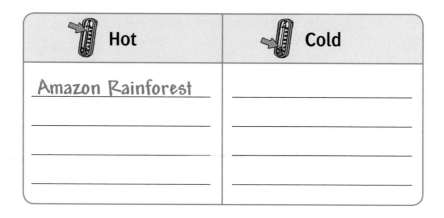

🌡 Hot	🌡 Cold
Amazon Rainforest	_____
_____	_____
_____	_____
_____	_____

3 **Order the words.**

1 move / slowly. / Glaciers / very

Glaciers move very slowly.

2 are / made / ice. / rivers / Glaciers / of

_____

3 dangerous / Icebergs / boats. / are / for

_____

4 of / the / Ilulissat / one / is / places. / coldest

_____

4 **Complete the questions. Then write the answers.**

How   What   ~~When~~   Where   Why

1 _When_ do glaciers begin?

They begin when snow falls.

2 _____ are glaciers made of?

_____

3 _____ are icebergs dangerous?

_____

4 _____ is Ilulissat?

_____

5 _____ long is the glacier at Ilulissat?

_____

5 Hot Water

← Read pages 12–13.

1 Write the words.

geyser   pool   rain   snow   steam   waterfall

1 _____   2 _____   3 _____

4 _____   5 _____   6 _____

2 Write *true* or *false*.

1 Geysers are made of water and steam.   _____

2 Geysers are usually very cold.   _____

3 Geysers look like big icebergs.   _____

4 The water in a geyser stays in the ground.   _____

5 Some monkeys in Japan sit in warm water.   _____

6 The cliffs at Pamukkale are very old.   _____

3 Match.

1 Under a geyser there is

2 Geysers make

3 The water in a geyser is

4 Don't

5 The cliffs at Pamukkale look like

6 Pamukkale is in

go near a geyser.

very hot.

waterfalls.

a loud noise.

a lot of hot rock.

Turkey.

4 Add the words and write correct sentences.

1 Deep under the, there is hot rock. (ground)

_____

2 When boils, it makes steam. (water)

_____

3 The monkeys at Jigokudani in the warm water. (sit)

_____

4 In the water there are. (minerals)

_____

5 The at Pamukkale look like waterfalls. (cliffs)

_____

6 Don't go near because they are very hot. (geysers)

_____

6 Mountains and Lakes

← Read pages 14–15.

1 Complete the sentences.

> deepest   highest   rivers
> mountain chain   moved   slowly

1 The Himalayas are a _____ in Asia.

2 Pieces of Earth's crust _____ and made the Himalayas.

3 The Himalayas are moving very _____.

4 Mount Everest is the _____ mountain in the world.

5 The _____ lake in the world is in Russia.

6 Water from 330 _____ goes into Lake Baikal.

2 Circle the odd one out.

1 fish   water   bird   snake

2 highest   longest   rainforest   biggest

3 mountain   lake   pond   river

4 moved   made   went   top

5 high   very   deep   big

6 Russia   Japan   Earth   Turkey

3 Write the questions. Then write the answers.

1 high / mountain in the world

   What is the highest mountain in the world?

   _____

2 deep / lake in the world

   _____

   _____

3 big / mountain chain in the world

   _____

   _____

4 big / river in the world

   _____

   _____

4 Answer the questions.

1 What is the highest mountain in your country?

   _____

2 What is the biggest lake in your country?

   _____

3 What is the most incredible place in your country?

   _____

   _____

7 Caves

← Read pages 16–17.

1 Circle the correct words.

1 There are sometimes caves **on** / **near** the coast.

2 Glaciers **move** / **break** and make caves.

3 The rain makes **caves** / **waves** in limestone.

4 The Sarawak Chamber is in **Brazil** / **Borneo**.

5 Stalactites are made of **ice** / **rock**.

6 People drew **pictures** / **paper** on the cave walls.

2 Order the words.

1 usually / Caves / wet. / are

_____

2 is / soft / a / Limestone / rock.

_____

3 often / in / limestone. / There / caves / are

_____

4 drew / walls. / People / pictures / cave / on

_____

5 people / Now / caves. / live / in / don't / most

_____

3 **Match and write the questions. Then write the answers.**

Where is

Is limestone very

Are caves

What are stalactites

Why did people

Do you

hard?

like caves?

made of?

the Sarawak Chamber?

draw on cave walls?

usually wet?

1 Where is the Sarawak Chamber?

It's in Borneo.

2 _____

_____

3 _____

_____

4 _____

_____

5 _____

_____

6 _____

_____

8 Earthquakes and Tsunamis

← Read pages 18–19.

1 Find and write.

c	b	u	i	l	d	i	n	g	f
t	s	u	n	a	m	i	e	y	h
w	h	s	z	t	d	g	o	m	o
b	g	t	r	e	e	m	c	i	u
v	w	q	b	l	w	z	e	u	s
e	a	r	t	h	q	u	a	k	e
s	v	d	f	y	x	c	n	p	c
c	e	f	l	o	o	d	w	l	k

1 _____   3 _____   5 _____   7 _____

2 _____   4 _____   6 _____   8 _____

2 Complete the sentences.

> buildings   in   moves   ocean   under

1 Usually Earth's crust _____ very slowly.

2 When there is an earthquake _____ fall down.

3 There are earthquakes _____ the ocean.

4 Earthquakes under the _____ sometimes make tsunamis.

5 The tsunami _____ 2004 was very big.

3 **Write *true* or *false*.**

1 Earth's crust moves a few kilometers
   every day.   _____

2 Earthquakes are dangerous.   _____

3 In an earthquake, it's a good idea
   to go under a heavy table.   _____

4 There are never earthquakes under
   the ocean.   _____

5 Earthquakes under the ocean are not
   usually dangerous.   _____

6 A tsunami is a small wave.   _____

4 **Correct the sentences.**

1 Earth's crust moves a few millimeters every day.

   _____

2 Big earthquakes are not very dangerous.

   _____

3 Earthquakes under the ground sometimes
   make tsunamis.

   _____

4 A tsunami is a giant building.

   _____

5 After a tsunami, there are often people.

   _____

9 Deserts

← Read pages 20–21.

1 Complete the puzzle.

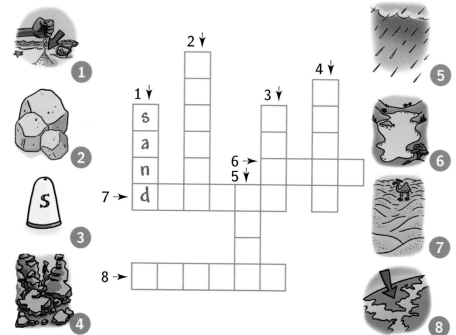

2 Match.

1 Some deserts are made	than Australia.
2 It doesn't rain often	made of salt.
3 The Sahara Desert is bigger	of sand.
4 Animals in the desert	in Antarctica.
5 In Bolivia, there is a desert	don't drink very often.
6 The Salar de Uyuni is	an incredible place.

3 Order the words.

1 usually / Deserts / hot. / are

_____

2 very / are / places. / dry / Deserts

_____

3 Africa. / The / in / is / Desert / Sahara

_____

4 Antarctica. / It's / in / cold / very

_____

5 visit / Salar de Uyuni. / people / Many / the

_____

4 Complete the questions. Then write the answers.

What   How much   Why   Where

1 _____ of the land on Earth is desert?

_____

2 _____ is the biggest hot desert on Earth?

_____

3 _____ is Bolivia?

_____

4 _____ do many people visit the Salar de Uyuni?

_____

10 Erosion

← Read pages 22–23.

1 Match and write the questions. Then write the answers.

Where is	Canyon?
What changed the	begin in the Colorado River?
Where is the Grand	Cappadocia?
What is the name of the river	in the Grand Canyon?
When did erosion	rocks in Cappadocia?

1 _____

_____

2 _____

_____

3 _____

_____

4 _____

_____

5 _____

_____

2 Complete the puzzle.

1 The monkeys in Jigokudani sit in the warm __.
2 __ under the ocean sometimes make tsunamis.
3 In South America there's a __ made of salt.
4 You can find incredible __ in limestone.
5 A __ is a hole in Earth's crust.
6 The Great Barrier Reef is near __.
7 The deepest __ in the world is in Russia.
8 A __ is a river made of ice.
9 The water in a __ is very hot.
10 All rivers go to the __.

3 **What do you think is the most incredible place on Earth? Why?** _____

_____

_____

1 Imagine your country 10,000 years ago. What was there? Write ✓ or ✗. Then write notes.

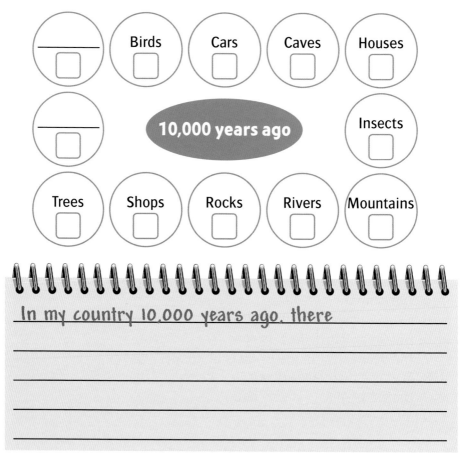

Birds Cars Caves Houses

10,000 years ago Insects

Trees Shops Rocks Rivers Mountains

In my country 10,000 years ago, there

_____

_____

_____

_____

2 Make a poster. Write about your country 10,000 years ago and draw some pictures.

3 Display your poster.

Project 2 Incredible Places in My Country

1 Complete the chart about incredible places in your country.

My country: _____

	Where is it?	What can you see?
The highest place: _____		
The longest river: _____		
The most beautiful place: _____		
The most incredible place: _____		

2 Find a photo or a picture of one of these places.

3 Make a poster. Write sentences to describe the incredible place. Display your poster.

Picture Dictionary

boil   coast   cover   dangerous   deep

desert   die   directions   Earth   earthquake

fall   flood   ground   hole   island

lake   loud   melt   million   minerals

| mountain chain | noise | ocean | pour | rainforest |

| river | road | rocks | salt | sand |

   stones stream

| sculpture | skin | steam | stones | stream |

  volcano

| submarine | top | valley | volcano | wave |

Oxford Read and Discover

Series Editor: Hazel Geatches • CLIL Adviser: John Clegg

Oxford Read and Discover graded readers are at six levels, for students from age 6 and older. They cover many topics within three subject areas, and support English across the curriculum, or Content and Language Integrated Learning (CLIL).

Available for each reader:
• Audio CD Pack (book & audio CD)
• Activity Book

Teaching notes & CLIL guidance: **www.oup.com/elt/teacher/readanddiscover**

Subject Area / Level	The World of Science & Technology	The Natural World	The World of Arts & Social Studies
1 300 headwords	• Eyes • Fruit • Trees • Wheels	• At the Beach • In the Sky • Wild Cats • Young Animals	• Art • Schools
2 450 headwords	• Electricity • Plastic • Sunny and Rainy • Your Body	• Camouflage • Earth • Farms • In the Mountains	• Cities • Jobs
3 600 headwords	• How We Make Products • Sound and Music • Super Structures • Your Five Senses	• Amazing Minibeasts • Animals in the Air • Life in Rainforests • Wonderful Water	• Festivals Around the World • Free Time Around the World
4 750 headwords	• All About Plants • How to Stay Healthy • Machines Then and Now • Why We Recycle	• All About Desert Life • All About Ocean Life • Animals at Night • Incredible Earth	• Animals in Art • Wonders of the Past
5 900 headwords	• Materials to Products • Medicine Then and Now • Transportation Then and Now • Wild Weather	• All About Islands • Animal Life Cycles • Exploring Our World • Great Migrations	• Homes Around the World • Our World in Art
6 1,050 headwords	• Cells and Microbes • Clothes Then and Now • Incredible Energy • Your Amazing Body	• All About Space • Caring for Our Planet • Earth Then and Now • Wonderful Ecosystems	• Food Around the World • Helping Around the World